PARACORD 101
A BEGINNER'S GUIDE TO PARACORD BRACELETS AND PROJECTS

TODD MIKKELSEN

Copyright © 2012 by Todd Mikkelsen. All Rights Reserved.

No part of this document may be reproduced or transmitted in any form or by any means, electronic, mechanical, photocopying, recording, or otherwise, without prior written permission of Todd Mikkelsen, except by a reviewer, who may quote short passages in a review where suitable credit is given.

Preface

Life has its ways of shutting doors and opening new ones for you. I was a science teacher for 14 years. I taught everything from computers, math, and science. I earned a BA in Earth Science Education and a Masters in Education with a Physics emphasis. I used project based activities such as water bottle rockets and mouse trap cars to help students understand basic scientific concepts. The door to the world of education closed. Another door opened for me when I tried to teach my two daughters how to make paracord bracelets in the summer of 2011. Neither one showed much interest in making bracelets at the time but they still wore them. My oldest daughter wore the paracord bracelets to middle school and several of her friends wanted one. Those friends told their friends where they got the bracelets. So, demand turned into a business.

You can see my knowledge gained through trial and error at:

http://www.etsy.com/shop/Tcords

http://paracord101.blogspot.com/

http://www.youtube.com/channel/UCzNmsPNlNnVH7wCr9gs6PLA

All of the information here can be easily found on the internet. However, I have always found it nice to have a hard copy of basic information. Why? The internet may go down and you will not have access to information to refer to. You may be sitting on your couch making bracelets and you can't remember the next step. This is when it is nice to have a book sitting next to you on a tablet or in paperback.

Table of Contents

Chapter 1 – What Do You Need? _____1

Chapter 2 – Paracord Prep and the Cobra Weave Bracelet_____7

Chapter 3 – Two Color Splicing_____14

    Part 1 – Melt and Smash_____14

    Part 2 – Overlay and Stitch_____14

    Part 3 – Sleeve and Stitch_____15

Chapter 4 – Two Color Piranha Weave Bracelet_____19

Chapter 5 – The Millipede Weave Bracelet_____25

Chapter 6 – King Cobra Weave Key Fob and Diamond Knot_____29

Chapter 7 – Neck Lanyard with King Cobra Weave and Diamond Knot_____36

Chapter 8 – Paracord Necklace with a 3 Cord Braid_____43

Chapter 1 – What Do You Need?

If this is a hobby or a business and you want to make paracord bracelets, key fobs, and lanyards time and time again, you will need several tools that will assist you. These tools will reduce the time it takes to make them and help relieve the anxiety or frustration when working on a project. Most of the items listed in this chapter can be found on popular internet market places.

Keep in mind that these are the tools that I prefer to use. Other paracordists may have differing opinions. You will need the following items:

1. 550 Paracord
The standard for most paracord bracelets and accessories is 550, 7 strand core, paracord.

2. Paracord Jig
A paracord jig is used to help stabilize paracord so it is easier to work with and help minimize frustration.

3. Fid
A fid is used to thread paracord through several loops of paracord.

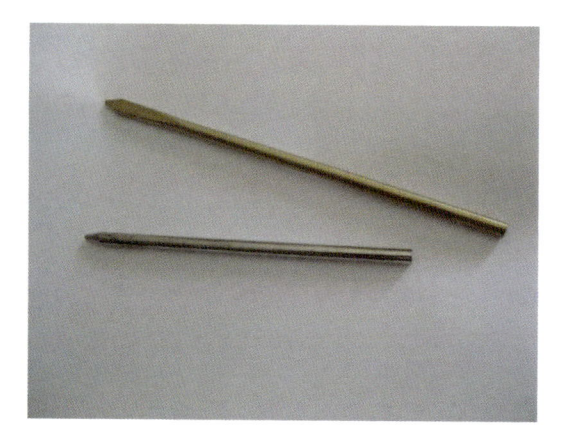

4. Threading Needles
Threading needles will be needed for mending two cords together.

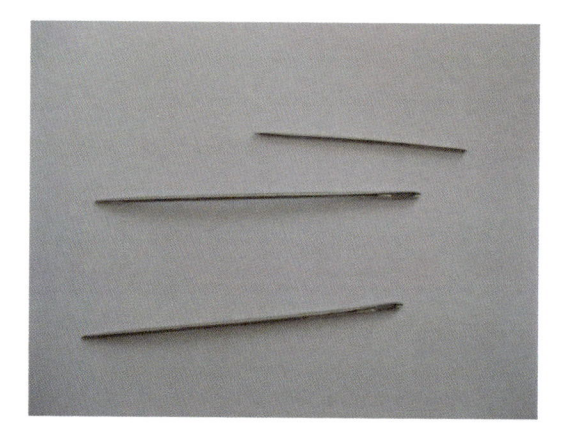

5. Thread or Fishing Line
Thread should be the same color as the cord. The transparent property of fishing line is useful to keep stitches hidden.

6. Lighter
A lighter is used to singe or melt the ends of the paracord.

7. Needle Nosed Pliers
Pliers can be used to help take apart a project due to an error or redo. The flat, non-textured, part of the pliers will be used to flatten the melted cord.

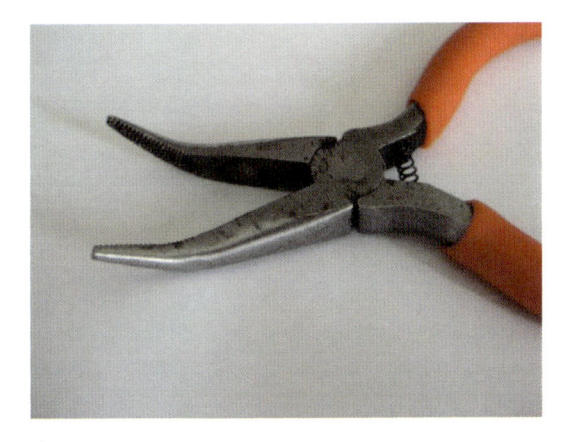

8. Forceps
Forceps are used similar to fids in pulling paracord through several loops.

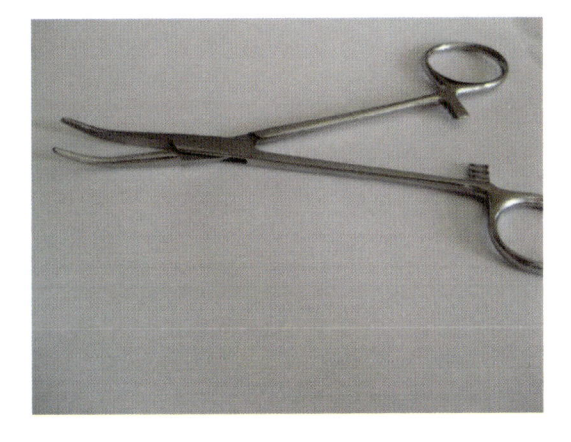

9. Scissors
Scissors will be used to cut paracord and thread.

10. Ruler, Yard Stick, or Measuring Tape
A ruler can be used to measure a paracord project.

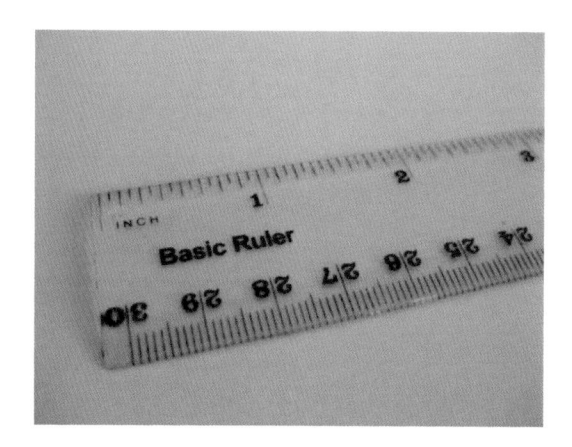

11. Garment Measuring Tape
A garment measuring tape should be used to measure a wrist, ankle, neck, etc.

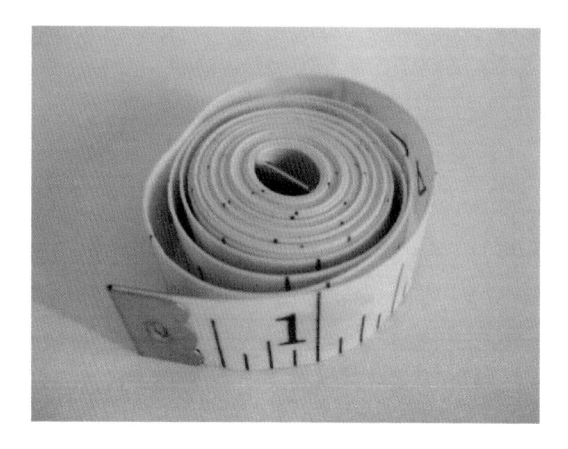

12. Buckles of Various Sizes
A typical paracord bracelet usually has a 3/8" or 5/8" buckle; stainless steel adjustable shackle is optional.

13. Plastic Containers
Plastic containers will keep tools organized.

14. Work Space
A work space will be needed to make paracord bracelets and to keep supplies within reach.

15. Notebook and pen

If you are going to make more than one bracelet and want to learn how to make them over and over, use a notebook and pen, or spreadsheet, to record how much paracord was used, type of buckle, knot, length of the bracelet, and excess paracord. Keeping track of data will help conserve paracord. Keep surplus scraps of paracord for future projects.

Chapter 2 – Paracord Prep and the Cobra Weave Bracelet

How much paracord will I need to use to make a bracelet? This is a touchy subject for most paracordists.

It depends on many factors: wrist size, buckle size, loose fit, tight fit, paracord width, etc. Some people like a loose fitting bracelet and others like a tight fitting bracelet. Some people like a small bracelet with only two strands of paracord in the core and some like to have four strands in the core… The list can go on and on. You will have to find what works for and record this information for future use.

The most basic and well known paracord bracelet uses the knot known as the Cobra Weave. Why is it called a Cobra Weave? Each loop looks like a snake's fang.

This project is designed for a 7 and 1/8 inch wrist. The paracord jig will need to be adjusted to roughly 2 inches longer than the size of my wrist for a comfortable fit. Adjust the paracord jig to 9 and 1/8 inches. 12 feet of paracord was cut to make this bracelet. The bracelet will have a four cord core and 5/8 inch buckle.

Prep the cord to make it easier to use when threading the buckles. After cutting the cord, make sure that there are no white strands sticking out. Trim the excess or make a new cut.

The next step is to melt the new end and smash it with the flat portion of the pliers' claw. Why do this? This will allow the paracord to be threaded through the buckle with ease.

Thread the buckle with the two flat ends of the paracord leaving a loop at the top of the buckle.

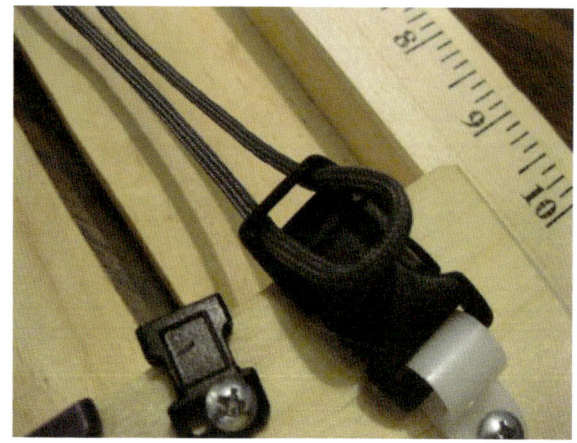

Next, thread the cord through the loop and tighten it.

The loop should now be at the bottom of the buckle and will be next to your wrist when wearing the bracelet. The loop will also be used to secure the ends of the cord once the project is finished.

Thread the cord through each buckle until there are four strands of cord in the core of the buckle.

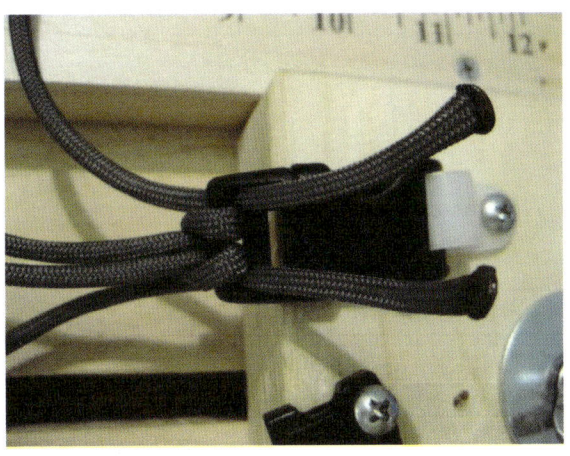

The first knot is critical to ensure a nice look for the bracelet. Start the Cobra Knot by making a loop with the left loose cord. The loose cord on the right is placed over the looped cord.

Take the cord on the right and loop it under the core, pull through the loop on the left, and tighten. The tighter the knot is the better the symmetry of all of the knots. If the knots are loose, the less symmetry for the bracelet.

Make a loop with the right loose cord. The loose cord on the left is placed over the looped cord.

Take the cord on the left and loop it under the core, pull through the loop on the right, and tighten.

Repeat these steps until the end of the paracord bracelet.

The last few steps are to ensure the quality, durability, and comfort of the bracelet. Unbuckle the bracelet from the jig. Take forceps or needle nose pliers and pull each end of paracord through the loop. A fid can also be used for this process. Simply cut the ends and attach the fid.

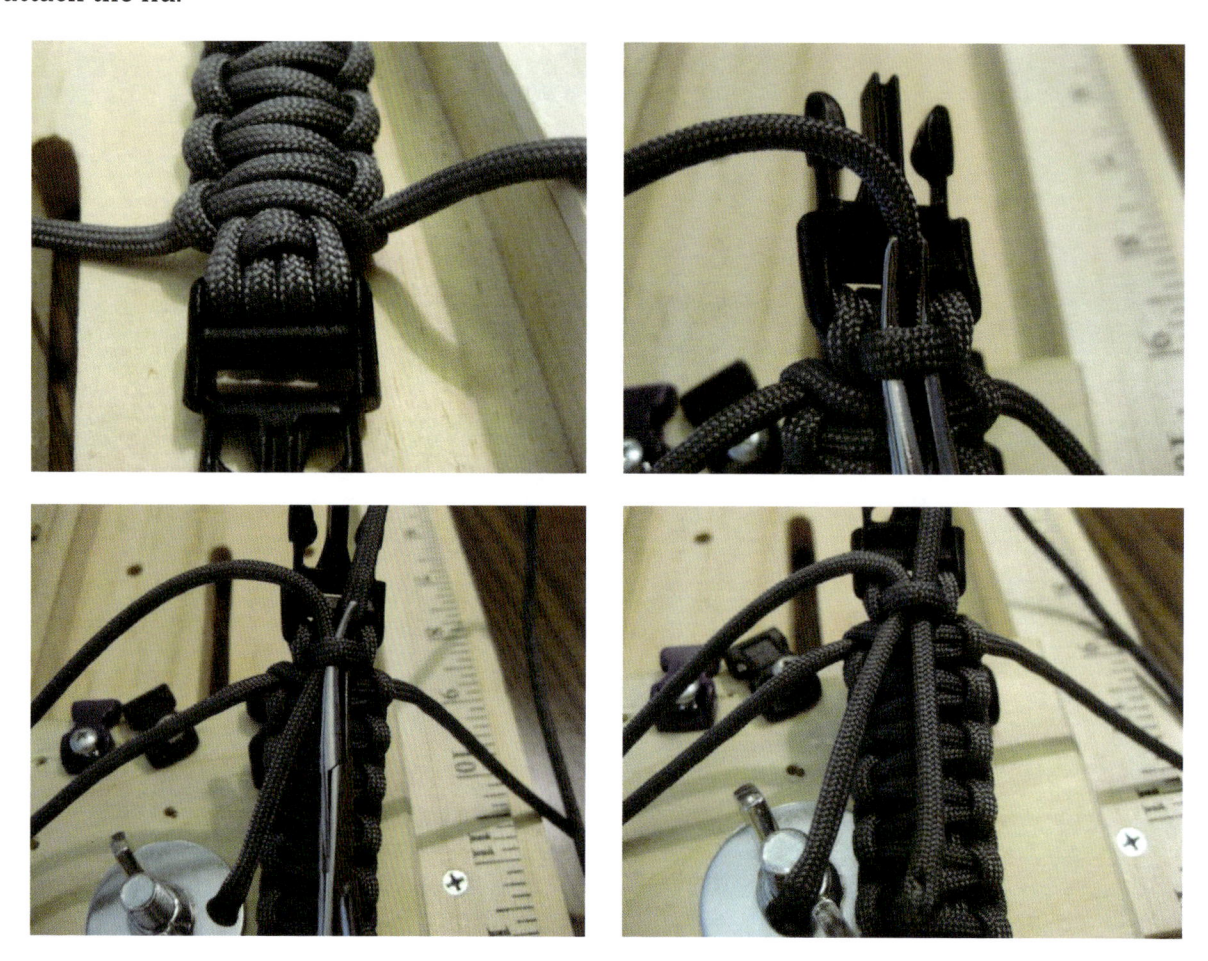

Try on the bracelet before this cut is made! Estimate 3/4 of an inch from the loop and cut.

Melt and smash the ends of the paracord. If the melted paracord is not smashed, it will leave a rounded edge; a rounded edge is difficult to thread through a buckle. While wearing the bracelet, the rounded edge will itch and be uncomfortable. Some popular paracord bracelet manufacturers skip the "smash" step to save time, and money, and leaving you with a $30 itchy paracord bracelet. A smashed edge is comfortable and does not itch if done properly.

The final result is shown below.

The main purpose for securing the two end strands through the loop is to ensure durability, stability, and quality. Several makers of paracord bracelets will singe the ends along the edge of the Cobra Weave. It is this paracordist's opinion that singeing paracord along the edge will damage the paracord. Damaged paracord will be of no use in an emergency situation. "Keep it secure, keep it safe," states this paracordist.

Chapter 3 – Two Color Splicing

There are several ways to splice paracord together. The method that is chosen will determine the quality of the bracelet that is produced.

Part 1 – Melt and Smash

The melt and smash method is the easiest way to splice or combine two different colors of paracord together. The drawback to this method is that it usually looks sloppy and will produce inconsistencies in the weave. The advantage to this method is that it will only take a minute to do.

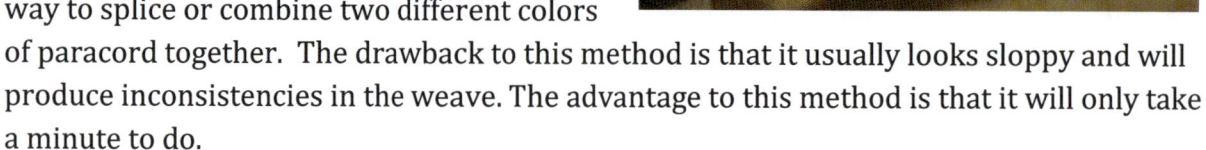

Part 2 – Overlay and Stitch

The overlay and stitch method is the second easiest way to merge two colors. First, melt and smash both ends of paracord. Second, trim the excess melt.

- 14 -

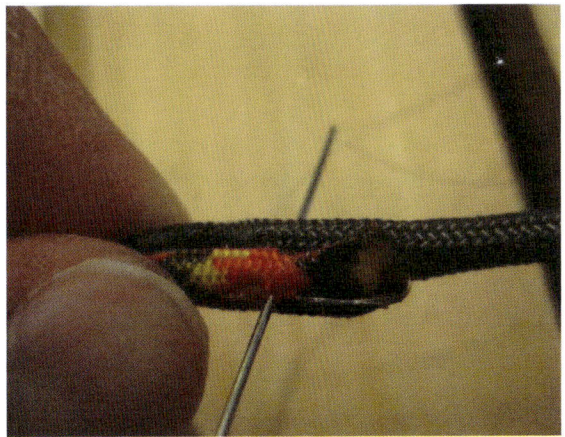

Third, lay two ends of paracord over each other and stitch the paracord together.

Part 3 – Sleeve and Stitch

The sleeve and stitch method is the most difficult. However, it will also appear the best if done right with lots of practice and patience. After cutting the paracord, pull roughly one inch of the seven-strand core out or the core and trim.

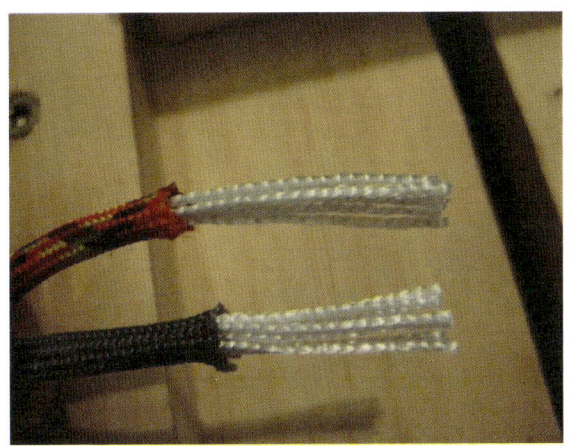

- 15 -

Next, pull the excess shell toward the open end to retract the seven-strand core into the shell.

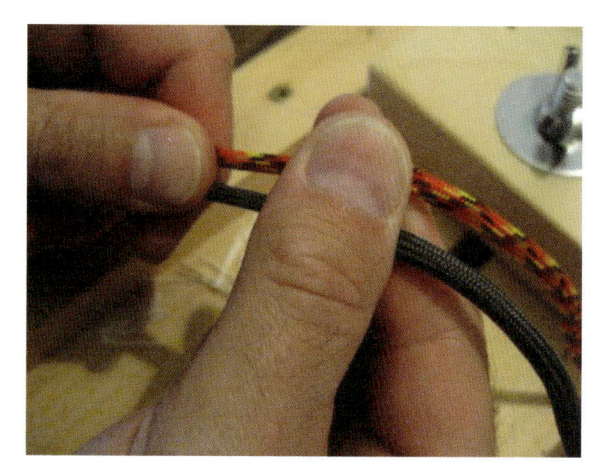

After that, singe one of the open ends, insert the forceps and open them to expand the paracord shell.

Next, the other paracord is cut at an angle, singed, smashed and trimmed to a point.

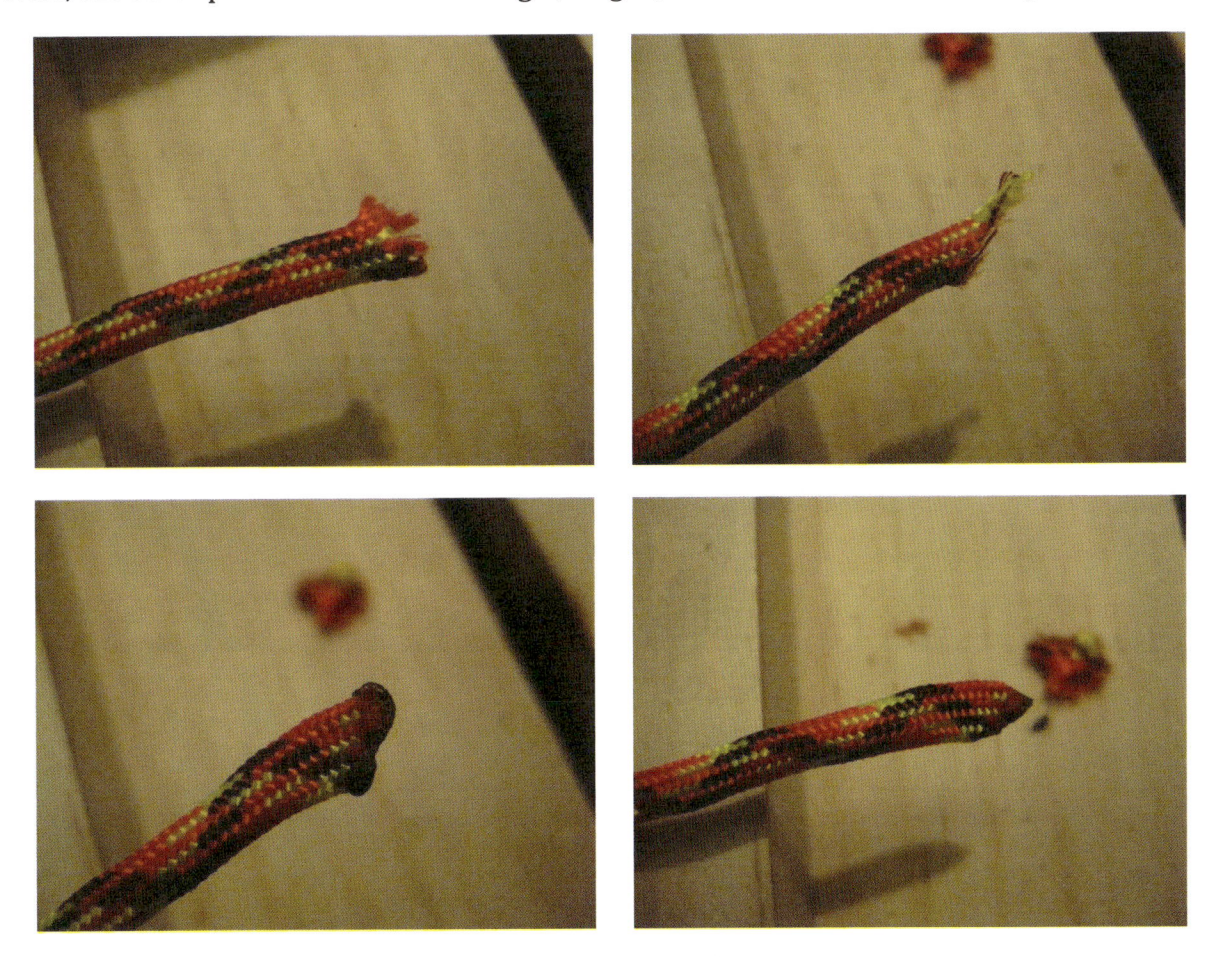

The paracord with a point is inserted into the paracord with the opening. Use the forceps to assist in pushing more paracord into the chamber.

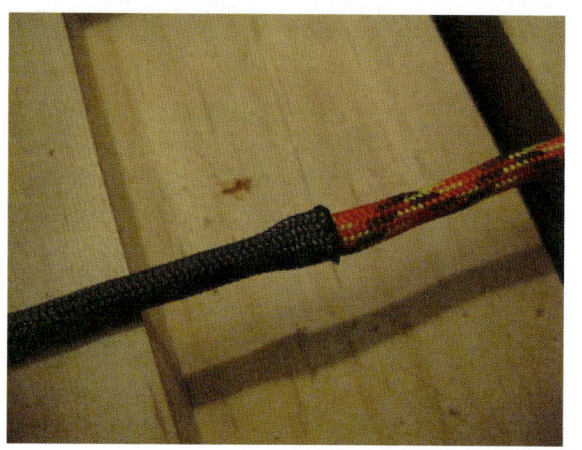

Lastly, stitch the paracord to aid the structural integrity of the paracord. The paracord is stitched multiple times to ensure that the two strands are secure and all of the paracord can be used during an emergency. Once the two strands together are sewn, give a good tug on both sides of the stitch to make sure it is secure.

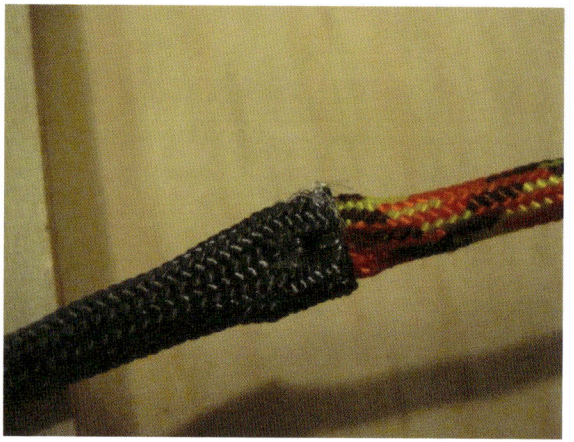

Chapter 4 – Two Color Piranha Weave Bracelet

This tutorial is going to demonstrate the Piranha Weave. It is assumed that prep paracord and two color paracord splice from the previous chapters are mastered.

This bracelet will be made for a 7 and 1/8 inch wrist. Two different colors of paracord strands of equal length have been spliced. 12 feet of paracord will be used to make this bracelet: six feet for each color. A 3/8 inch plastic buckle will be used.

The paracord jig is adjusted to 8 and 1/4 inches. With a two cord core and 3/8 inch buckle, 1 and 1/8 inches need to be added for a comfortable fit.

Insert both ends of the paracord to create a loop at the top. Next, take the two ends and pull them through the loop and tighten. The loop should now be at the bottom and will be used later.

The cord on the left is pulled between the two cord core and lies underneath the cord on the right. The paracord on the right is pulled between the two cord core and through the loop on the left and tightened.

Start with the left cord, or orange camouflage. It will be the base or the bottom color and will weave back and forth when making this bracelet. The right cord, or charcoal grey paracord, will be the top color.

For the second step, pull the orange camouflage paracord between the two core strands. Next, the charcoal grey paracord is pulled between the two core strands, through the loop of the camouflage paracord and tightened.

The process is repeated.

Continue the weave to the end of the bracelet.

Detach the bracelet and pull the charcoal grey, right, paracord through the two cord core with forceps. This is done to keep the Piranha Weave pattern on the top of the bracelet.

To secure the paracord into place, loop both ends through the main loop and tighten.

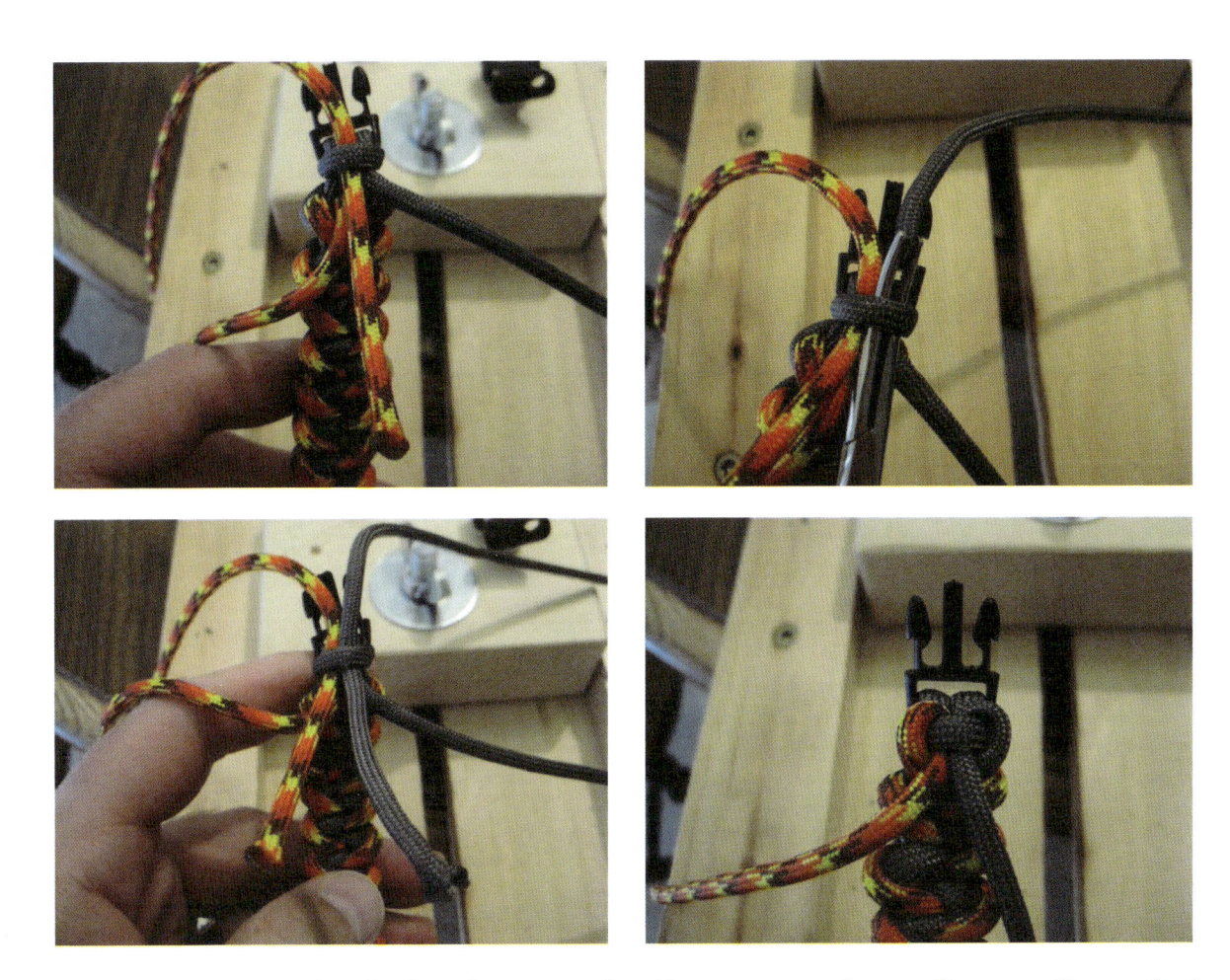

Before the bracelet is finished, make sure it fits. If not, get out the needle nose pliers, take it apart, readjust the paracord jig, and start again.

If it does fit, estimate 3/4 of an inch from the main loop, cut, melt and smash.

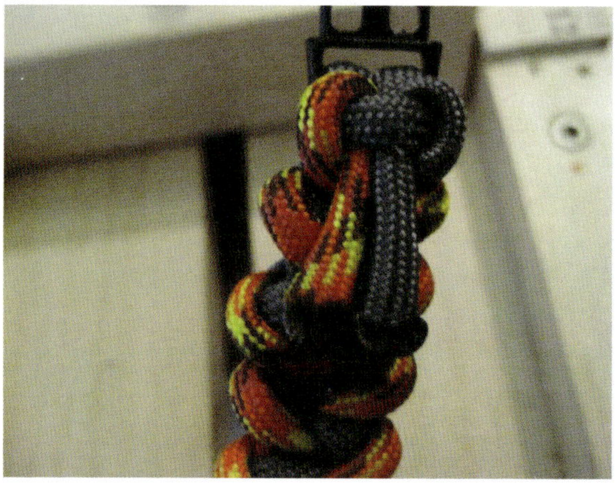 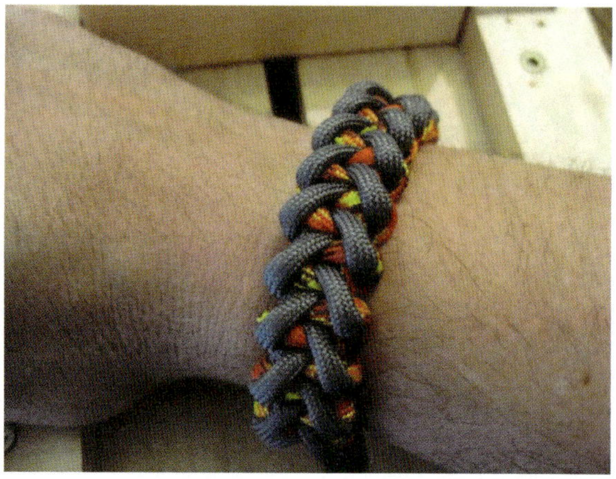

Chapter 5 – The Millipede Weave Bracelet

This tutorial will show the Millipede Weave. It is easy to make and easy to put back together once it is used. Two different colors of paracord will be shown for contrast. Two six feet sections are spliced creating one 12 feet strand of paracord.

It is assumed, again, that paracord prep and the two color splice is mastered from prior chapters.

The bracelet will be made for a 7 and 1/8 inch wrist with a 3/8 inch plastic buckle. The paracord strands are spliced and a two strand core will be the center of the bracelet.

The paracord jig is adjusted to 8 and 1/4 inches. From experience, a two cord core and 3/8 inch buckle will require roughly 1 and 1/8 inches for a good fit.

Loop the left, grey, paracord under the two strand core, through the loop of the left paracord creating an overhand knot, and tighten.

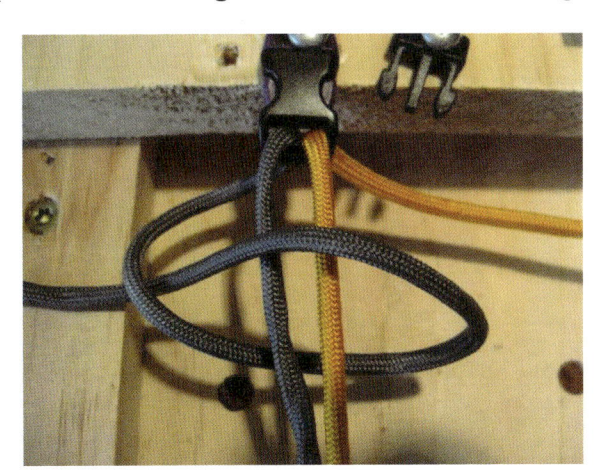

The process is repeated with the right, yellow, paracord. Loop the right strand under the two strand core and through the loop of the yellow strand creating an overhand knot. Tighten the knot.

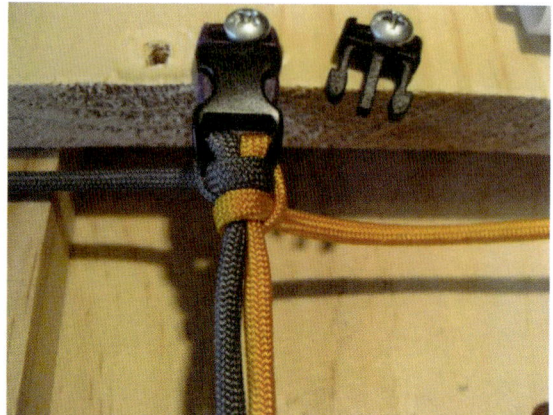

The left, charcoal grey, paracord knot is pulled over and underneath the two strand core, threaded back through the left cord, and tighten.

After that, the right, yellow, paracord knot is pulled over and underneath the two strand core, looped back through the right cord, and tighten the cord.

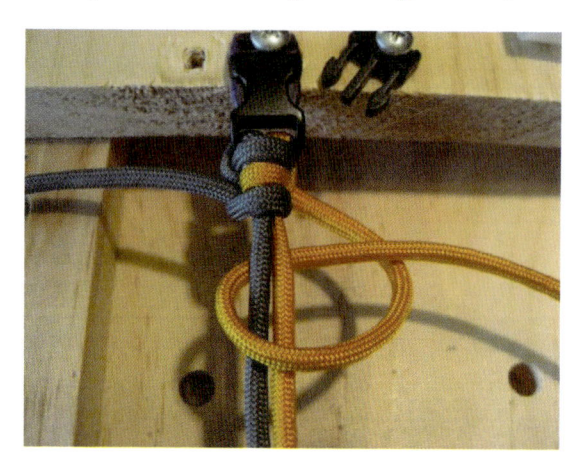

This process is repeated until the end of the bracelet.

Detach the bracelet, pull both ends through the end loop with forceps and tighten.

Check to see if the bracelet fits.

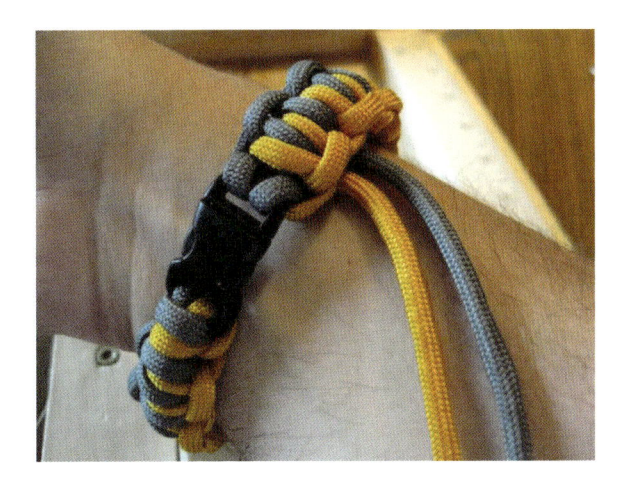

Estimate 3/4 of an inch, cut, melt, and smash.

Chapter 6 – King Cobra Weave Key Fob and Diamond Knot

A key fob is a great way to keep track of keys. The key fob tutorial can also be adapted to a luggage tag. Simply make the first loop longer so it can be looped around a luggage handle. Another use for the key fob is to attach it to a knife or another tool.

This tutorial will use seven feet of paracord. A King Cobra weave will be used in this project. A King Cobra weave is simply two layers of paracord made with a Cobra Weave.

Make a bend half way.

Next, loop the paracord to make a simple knot and tighten.

- 29 -

This key fob will be four inches long. Take both sides and weave each into the other. The right cord is pulled underneath the cord on the left. The cord on the left is pulled underneath the cord on the right. This should be the start of the Cobra Weave.

The cord on the left loops over the core pulls through the loop on the right that goes under the core. The cord on the right is pulled through the left loop. Tighten it.

Make a loop with the right cord over the two cord core. The loose cord on the left is pulled under the two cord core. Pull the left cord through the loop on the right and tighten.

Repeat these steps until the end of the key fob.

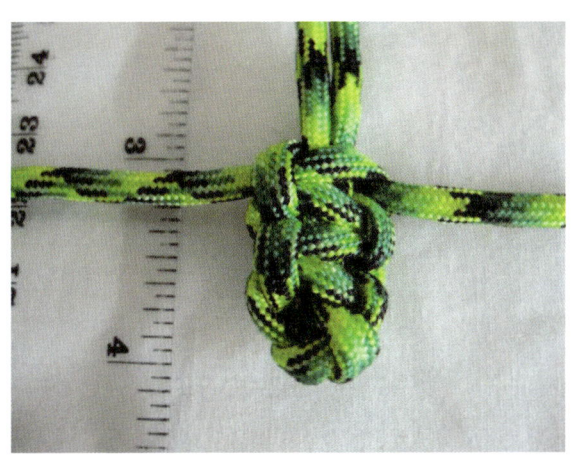

Start the King Cobra Weave on top of what is now the Cobra Weave Core and continue until the end of the key fob.

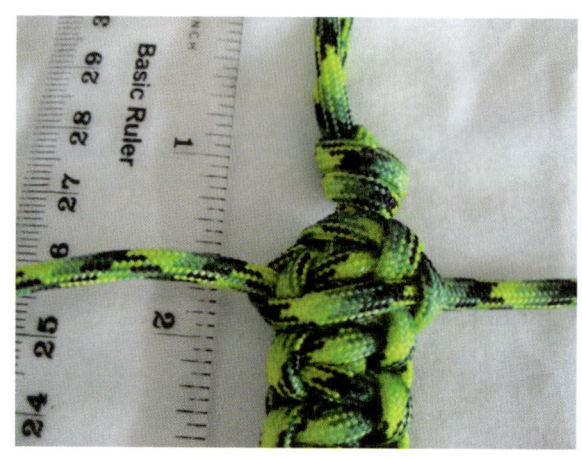

The diamond knot starts with a loop. The right cord loops under itself to start the knot.

The left cord is a bend through the right cord.

The remainder of the left cord is looped around and underneath the right cord. Then, it is looped underneath the loop created in the prior image.

The knot is slightly tightened and curved to start the formation of the diamond knot.

The cord on the left is looped around the base cord on the right in a counter-clockwise direction and is pulled through the center of the knot.

The cord on the right is looped around the base cord on the left in a counter-clockwise direction and is pulled through the center of the knot.

Tighten the knot, cut the cord, and singe the ends. Use needle nose pliers to adjust and center the knot if needed.

Chapter 7 – Neck Lanyard with King Cobra Weave and Diamond Knot

A paracord neck lanyard has many uses. It can hold an I.D. badge, whistle, duck call, compass, G.P.S., bottle opener, survival gear, etc.

Neck lanyards can be made out of any color and can be customized the same as any other paracord project. Inspiration can come from a favorite team's colors, corporate colors, camouflage for hunting, or neutral color, or colors, for the everyday wardrobe.

This project will use two separate strands of the same color. One strand of paracord will be four feet and the other will be ten feet. A lobster claw clasp will be used in this lanyard.

The shorter of the two cords is used for the neck piece. Bend the cord in half and loop it through the clasp and pull the two strands back through the loop. Do not tighten the cord.

The longer of the two strands is pulled through the loop to its mid-point.

- 36 -

The shorter of the two strands, the neck piece, is tightened to secure the two cords.

A simple knot can be made at the end of the shorter cord to keep it organized.

Start the Cobra Weave as shown in previous chapters.

Stop knotting once the desired length is reached. The weave will be six inches for this project.

Start the King Cobra Weave and keep going until the clasp is reached.

Use forceps or a fid and pull the two ends through the loop made at the start of the project. For additional stability, loop through part of the Cobra Weave as well. Use needle nose pliers to retighten the loosened cord in the weave.

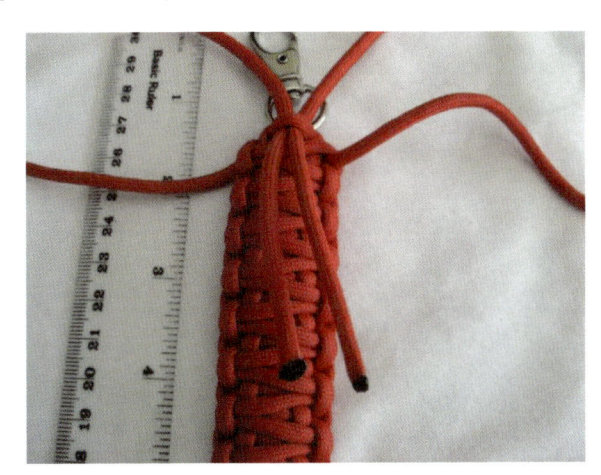

The diamond knot starts with a loop. The right cord loops under itself to start the knot and the left cord has a bend through to right cord.

The rest of the left cord is looped around and under the right cord. Then, it is loops beneath the loop.

The knot is slightly tightened and curved to start the formation of the diamond knot.

The cord on the left is looped around the base cord on the right in a counter-clockwise direction and is pulled through the center of the knot.

The cord on the right is looped around the base cord on the left in a counter-clockwise direction and is pulled through the center of the knot.

Tighten the knot, cut excess cord and singe the ends. Adjust and center the knot if needed.

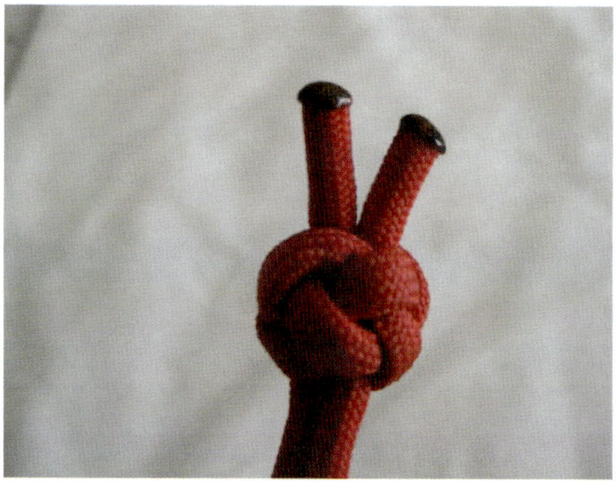

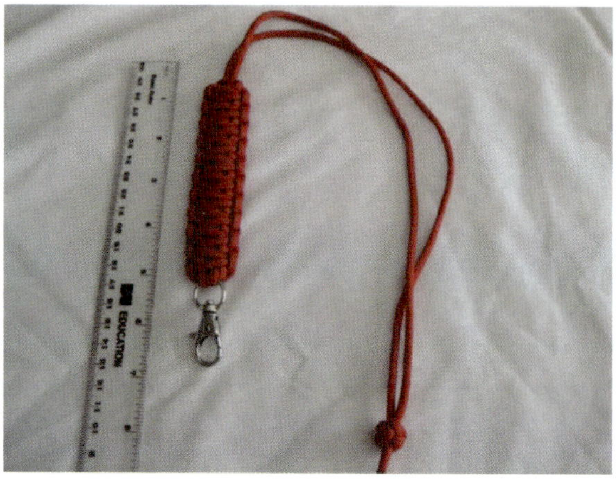

Chapter 8 – Paracord Necklace with a 3 cord Braid

A paracord necklace can be used to show support for a favorite team, attach a survival whistle, a compass, etc.

A paracord necklace can be created by cutting three, four feet sections of paracord. Three different colors are used in this project for contrast.

Two cords will be placed on top of each other. Choose one of them and roughly make a one inch loop. Use forceps to lock both cords into place. The third cord will lie next to the other two.

The third cord is looped several times around the two clamped cords. Make three to four loops.

Take the opposite end of the looping cord and thread it through the middle.

Slowly tighten and adjust the knot until the cord is tight.

- 44 -

Start the three cord braid by moving two cords to the right and leave one cord on the left.

A cord from either edge, or side, will be placed on top in an alternating pattern. The cord on the right is placed over the middle cord.

The cord on the left is placed over the middle cord and the knot is tightened.

Continue this alternating pattern until the desired length is reached.

Forceps are used to keep the knot from loosening.

Choose any of the three cords and begin to loop it around all three cords.

The loose end of the looped cord is threaded through the center opening.

Tighten and adjust the cord as needed.

As shown in previous chapters, a diamond knot is created to secure the necklace for use.

The third cord is pulled through the center of the knot. All three cords should be in the middle of the knot.

The diamond knot is tightened and adjusted with pliers.

Cut and singe the paracord.

The excess cord is cut from the loop that the diamond knot will use to secure the necklace.

Fold the loop for easy access to singe the ends.

The looped cord is adjusted to help lock the diamond knot into place. The excess is trimmed and singed.

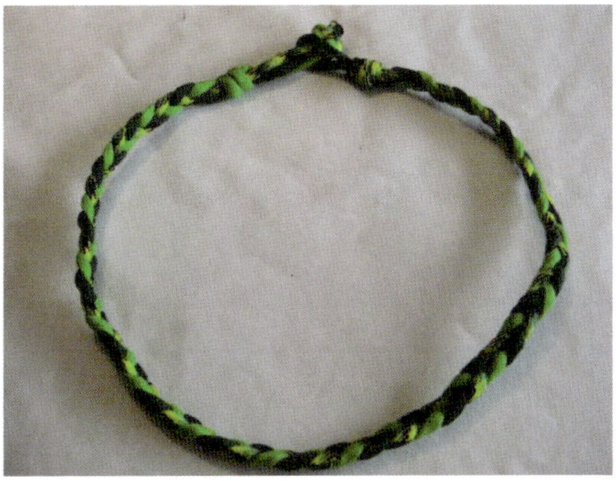

Made in the USA
San Bernardino, CA
27 June 2013